85 Meal and Juice Recipes to Lower Your High Blood Pressure:

Solve Your Hypertension Problem in 12 Days or Less!

By

Joseph Correa

Certified Sports Nutritionist

COPYRIGHT

© 2016 Finibi Inc

All rights reserved

Reproduction or translation of any part of this work beyond that permitted by section 107 or 108 of the 1976 United States Copyright Act without the permission of the copyright owner is unlawful.

This publication is designed to provide accurate and authoritative information in regard to the subject matter covered. It is sold with the understanding that neither the author nor the publisher is engaged in rendering medical advice. If medical advice or assistance is needed, consult with a doctor. This book is considered a guide and should not be used in any way detrimental to your health. Consult with a physician before starting this nutritional plan to make sure it's right for you.

ACKNOWLEDGEMENTS

The realization and success of this book could not have been possible without the motivation and support of my entire family.

85 Meal and Juice Recipes to Lower Your High Blood Pressure:

Solve Your Hypertension Problem in 12 Days or Less!

By

Joseph Correa

Certified Sports Nutritionist

CONTENTS

Copyright

Acknowledgements

About The Author

Introduction

What Is High Blood Pressure?

How Do You Manage High Blood Pressure?

Calendar to Lower Your Blood Pressure

Meal Recipes to Lower Your Blood Pressure

Juice Recipes to Lower Your Blood Pressure

Other Great Titles by This Author

ABOUT THE AUTHOR

As a certified sports nutritionist, I honestly believe in the positive effects that proper nutrition can have over the body and mind. My knowledge and experience has helped me live healthier throughout the years and which I have shared with family and friends. The more you know about eating and drinking healthier, the sooner you will want to change your life and eating habits.

Nutrition is a key part in the process of being healthy and living longer so get started today.

INTRODUCTION

85 Meal and Juice Recipes to Lower Your High Blood Pressure will help you to control your blood pressure better naturally and fast. Hypertension is a serious health problem that should be addressed with exercise and proper nutrition. These are not to replace meals but should complement your normal day to day meals.

Being too busy to eat right can sometimes become a problem and that's why this book will save you time and help nourish your body to achieve the goals you want.

This book will help you to:

-Control your high blood pressure

-Faster process by adding meals and juices to control blood pressure levels.

-Reduce Fat.

-Cleanse Your Blood Stream.

-Have more energy.

-Naturally accelerate Your Metabolism to become thinner.

-Improve your digestive system.

Joseph Correa is a certified sports nutritionist and a professional athlete.

WHAT IS HIGH BLOOD PRESSURE?

Blood pressure is the force of blood against the walls of the arteries. Under normal circumstances blood pressure rises and falls throughout the day. However, when it stays elevated over time, it is called high blood pressure.

The medical term for high blood pressure is hypertension. A blood pressure over 140/90 mmHg falls into the category of hypertension, while one between 120/80 mmHg and 139/89 mmHg refers to prehypertension, which can rapidly turn into hypertension if measures are not taken. There are certain risk factors that cannot be controlled, such as age (55 or older for men and 65 or older for women), and a history of early heart disease. The ones that can be controlled are an elevated blood pressure, diabetes, weight, physical activity, cholesterol levels and tobacco use and these are the risk factors targeted by medication and lifestyle changes.

HOW DO YOU MANAGE HIGH BLOOD PRESSURE?

Since high blood pressure contributes to atherosclerosis, heart disease, stroke, kidney disease and blindness, it becomes imperative to manage it effectively, through proper medication and lifestyle changes.

Having a proper diet is important to managing high blood pressure. It can help you lose weight or stay at a healthy weight, get the minerals and vitamins your body requires, and help you lower your blood pressure.

So, what should you eat? Foods that are lower in saturated fat and cholesterol should be a priority. Get your healthy fats with fish, such as salmon, nuts and olive oil. Make sure that your meals include whole wheat grains, poultry, fish, nuts, low fat dairy, and shy away from sugared beverages, sweets and high fat red meats.

An important part of healthy eating is choosing foods that are low in salt and other forms of sodium. Using less sodium is key to keeping blood pressure at a healthy level. For someone with a blood pressure controlled with medication, the maximum daily recommended amount is of 6 grams (about 1 teaspoon) of table salt a day. So you don't have to completely cut salt out of your diet, but make sure to reduce it as much as possible and give flavor to your food by experimenting with spices and herbs.

Try the following recipes and enjoy meal plan that will keep your blood pressure in check.

CALENDAR TO LOWER YOUR BLOOD PRESSURE

Week 1:

Day 1:

Lemon and Blueberry Pancakes

Snack: Smoothie

Rosemary Roasted Chicken Thighs

Snack: Cup of Popcorn

Lentil Dhal with Eggplant

Day 2:

Feta and Semi-Dried Tomato Omelette

Snack: Trail Mix

Beef Stew

Snack: Blueberry Yogurt

Spicy Spaghetti

Day 3:

Banana Bread

Snack: Avocado on Toast

Ratatouille Chicken

Snack: Apple Crisps

Green Beans and Corn Cakes

Day 4:

Avocado and Turkey on Toast

Snack: Energy Nuggets

Minestrone

Snack: Grilled Asparagus

Pear and Blue Cheese Salad

Day 5:

Granola Bars

Snack: Soya Milk Smoothie

Chicken Curry with Peanut Butter

Snack: Cinnamon Oranges

Vegetable Tagine

Day 6:

Asparagus and Soft-Broiled Egg

Snack: Dried Apricot Bar

Salmon and Brown Rice Salad

Snack: Apple and Peanut Butter

Spiced Quinoa

Day 7:

Breakfast Smoothie

Snack: Roasted Chickpeas

Beef Cobbler

Snack: Strawberry Greek Yogurt

Rosemary Risotto

Week 2:

Day 1:

Baked Eggs with Vegetables

Snack: Cup of Popcorn

Spaghetti with Sardines

Snack: Smoothie

Grapefruit Salad

Day 2:

Creamy Porridge

Snack: Blueberry Yogurt

Steamed Bass with Cabbage

Snack: Trail Mix

Spinach and Tofu Cannelloni

Day 3:

Mustard Mushrooms on Toast

Snack: Apple Crisps

Chicken Salad

Snack: Avocado on Toast

Baked Polenta

Day 4:

Fruity Muffins

Snack: Grilled Asparagus

Salmon and Spinach

Snack: Energy Nuggets

Squash and Lentil Salad

Day 5:

Feta and Semi-Dried Tomato Omelette

Snack: Cinnamon Oranges

Tuna Salad

Snack: Soya Milk Smoothies

Vegetable Pie

Day 6:

Lemon and Blueberry Pancakes

Apple and Peanut Butter

Beef Stew

Snack: Dried Apricot Bar

Spicy Spaghetti

Day 7:

Avocado and Turkey on Toast

Snack: Strawberry Greek Yogurt

Rosemary Roasted Chicken Thighs

Snack: Roasted Chickpeas

Green Beans and Corn Cakes

Week 3:

Day 1:

Banana Bread

Snack: Smoothie

Chicken Salad

Snack: Trail Mix

Grapefruit Salad

Day 2:

Asparagus and Soft-Broiled Egg

Snack: Cup of Popcorn

Minestrone

Snack: Blueberry Yogurt

Lentil Dhal with Eggplant

Day 3:

Granola Bars

Snack: Apple Crisps

Ratatouille Chicken

Snack: Grilled Asparagus

Pear and Blue Cheese Salad

Day 4:

Baked Eggs with Vegetables

Snack: Avocado on Toast

Salmon and Brown Rice Salad

Snack: Energy Nuggets

Vegetable Tagine

Day 5:

Breakfast Smoothie

Snack: Cinnamon Oranges

Chicken Curry with Peanut Butter

Snack: Dried Apricot Bar

Spiced Quinoa

Day 6:

Mustard Mushrooms on Toast

Snack: Soya Milk Smoothie

Spaghetti with Sardines

Snack: Apple and Peanut Butter

Baked Polenta

Day 7:

Creamy Porridge

Snack: Strawberry Greek Yogurt

Beef Cobbler

Snack: Cup of Popcorn

Grapefruit Salad

Week 4:

Day 1:

Fruity Muffins

Snack: Roasted Chickpeas

Chicken Salad

Snack: Smoothie

Rosemary Risotto

Day 2:

Feta and Semi-Dried Tomato Omelette

Snack: Trail Mix

Steamed Bass with Cabbage

Snack: Blueberry Yogurt

Squash and Lentil Salad

Day 3:

Lemon and Blueberry pancakes

Snack: Avocado on Toast

Tuna Salad

Snack: Apple Crisps

Spinach and Tofu Cannelloni

Day 4:

Asparagus and Soft-Broiled Egg

Snack: Energy Nuggets

Salmon and Spinach

Snack: Grilled Asparagus

Spicy Spaghetti

Day 5:

Banana Bread

Snack: Cinnamon Oranges

Rosemary Roasted Chicken Thighs

Snack: Apple and Peanut Butter

Vegetable Tagine

Day 6:

Avocado and Turkey on Toast

Snack: Soya Milk Smoothie

Salmon and Brown Rice Salad

Snack: Dried Apricot Bar

Baked Polenta

Day 7:

Creamy Porridge

Snack: Cup of Popcorn

Beef Stew

Snack: Blueberry Yogurt

Pear and Blue Cheese Salad

MEAL RECIPES TO LOWER YOUR BLOOD PRESSURE

BREAKFAST

1. Lemon and Blueberry Pancakes

Treat yourself to a freshly-made batch of pancakes that will give your day a nice jump start. Complement the zesty berry flavor with a spoon of low-fat yogurt and a sprinkle of cinnamon.

Ingredients (7 pancakes):

100g whole wheat flour

100ml milk

1 small egg

40g blueberries

zest from ½ lemon

½ teaspoon cream of tartar

¼ teaspoon bicarbonate of soda

½ teaspoon golden syrup

butter, for cooking

Prep time: 10 min

Cooking time: 10 min

Preparation:

Mix the flour, cream of tartar and bicarbonate with a fork. Drop the golden syrup into the ingredients along with the lemon zest and blueberries.

Pour the milk into a cup, break in the egg and mix well with a fork. Pour most of the milk mixture into the bowl with the flour mix and mix well with a rubber spatula. Keep adding more milk until you get a thick, smooth batter.

Heat the frying pan and brush with a little butter, then spoon in the batter 1 tablespoon at a time. When bubbles appear on top of the pancakes, turn them with a spatula. Cook until brown. Keep the pancakes warm until you have used the entire batter then serve.

Nutritional value per pancake: 69kcal, 2g protein, 12g carbs (1g fiber, 2g sugar), 1g fat (1g saturated), 0.1g salt.

2. Mustard Mushrooms on Toast

High in nutrients, especially vitamin C, this healthy vegetarian breakfast takes only 10 min to make and is made tastier by a nice cream cheese mustard-flavored sauce.

Ingredients (2 servings):

6 handfuls small flat mushrooms, sliced

3 tablespoons light cream cheese

4 tablespoons skimmed milk

2 tablespoons rapeseed oil

2 tablespoons chives, snipped

½ tablespoon wholegrain mustard

2 slices whole wheat bread

300ml orange juice, freshly squeezed

Prep time: 5 min

Cooking time: 5 min

Preparation:

Toast the bread and spread with a little of the cheese.

Heat the oil in a non-stick pan and cook the mushrooms, stirring frequently. When the mushrooms have softened, add the milk, mustard and remaining cheese then stir until well coated.

Tip the mushrooms mix onto the toast, top with the chives and serve with the juice.

Nutritional value per serving: 231kcal, 13g protein, 28g carbs (4g fiber, 16g carbs), 7g fat (2g saturated), 0.1g salt, 10% calcium, 10% iron, 12% magnesium, 140% vitamin C, 14% vitamin E, 17% vitamin K, 24% vitamin B1, 63% vitamin B2, 49% vitamin B3, 18% vitamin B6, 20% vitamin B9.

3. Banana Bread

Low in fat and high in energy-boosting carbs, this healthy banana loaf is a perfect option for breakfast. Pair it with a glass of milk and add some bone-strengthening calcium to your diet.

Ingredients (10 slices):

100g self-rising flour

140g whole wheat flour

300g overripe bananas, mashed

3 large eggs, beaten

150g low-fat natural yogurt

4 tablespoons agave syrup

1 teaspoon baking powder

1 teaspoon bicarbonate of soda

a pinch of salt

low-fat spread, for the tin

Prep time: 20 min

Cooking time: 1h and 15 min

Preparation:

Heat the oven to 140C fan/gas 3. Grease and line a tin with baking parchment (allow it to come 2cm above the top of the tin).

Mix the flour, baking powder, bicarbonate and a pinch of salt in a large bowl.

Mix the bananas, eggs, yogurt and syrup then quickly stir into the dry ingredients. Gently scrape the batter into the tin. Bake for 1h and 15 min or until a fork comes out clean.

Slice the banana bread then serve warm or at room temperature.

Nutritional value per slice: 145kcal, 6g protein, 24g carbs (3g fiber, 9g sugar), 2g fat (1g saturated), 0.6g salt, 11% vitamin B1, 13% vitamin B9.

4. Asparagus and Soft-Broiled Egg

A quick breakfast with a vitamin K kick, that is high in filling protein and low in saturated fat. Serve next to a piece of whole wheat toast for an extra energy punch.

Ingredients (2 servings):

2 eggs

10 asparagus spears

25g fine dry breadcrumbs

1 teaspoon olive oil

a pinch of chili

a pinch of paprika

a pinch of sea salt

Prep time: 10 min

Cooking time: 10 min

Preparation:

Heat the oil in a non-stick pan, add the breadcrumbs and fry until crisp and golden. Season with the sea salt and spices then let it cool.

Cook the asparagus in a large pan of boiling water until tender. At the same time, boil the eggs for 4 min.

Put each egg in an egg cup on a plate, divide the asparagus between the plates, scatter with the crumbs and serve.

Nutritional value per serving: 186kcal, 12g protein, 12g carbs (2g fiber, 3g sugar), 10g fat (2g saturated), 0.75g salt, 18% iron, 14% vitamin A, 41% vitamin K, 28% vitamin B1, 20% vitamin B2, 15% vitamin B3, 18% vitamin B9, 10% vitamin B12.

5. Breakfast Smoothie

Try a fruit smoothie first thing in the morning if you want to boost your energy levels and pack some vitamins as well. The mango and passion fruit combination boasts exotic and complementing flavors.

Ingredients (2 servings):

1 banana, chopped

1 small mango, chopped

3 passion fruits

300ml orange juice, freshly squeezed

ice cubes

Prep time: 5 min

No cooking

Preparation:

Scoop the pulp of the passion fruits into a blender, add the mango, orange juice and banana and blend until smooth. Pour into 2 glasses and serve immediately topped with ice cubes.

Nutritional value per serving: 175kcal, 3g protein, 39g carbs (4g fiber, 30g sugar), 0.05g salt, 12% magnesium, 30% vitamin C, 14% vitamin B1, 10% vitamin B2, 22% vitamin B6, 20% vitamin B9.

6. Granola Bars

Try a granola bar if you're in a hurry in the morning and you need a little pick me up before work. At 30g carbs per bar, your energy requirements will surely be met, and your taste buds will enjoy the nut/fruit/seed mix.

Ingredients (6 bars):

100g porridge oats

50g butter, plus extra for greasing

50g sunflower seeds

25g walnuts, chopped

25g sesame seeds

50g dried cranberries

50g light muscavado sugar

1 ½ tablespoons honey

½ teaspoon cinnamon

Prep time: 15 min

Cooking time: 35 min

Preparation:

Heat the oven to 140C fan/ gas 3. Butter and line the base of a baking tin.

Mix the porridge oats, nuts and seeds in roasting tine then put it in the oven for 5 min.

Warm the butter, sugar and honey in a pan, stirring until the butter has melted. Add the oat mix, dried cranberries and cinnamon, then mix until the oats are well coated. Tip into the baking tin, press down lightly then bake for 30 min.

Let the mix cool in the tin then cut into 6 bars and serve.

Nutritional value per bar: 294kcal, 30g carbs (3g fiber, 17g sugar), 17g fat (6g saturated), 0.15g salt, 10% iron, 15% vitamin E, 15% vitamin B1.

7. Baked Eggs with Vegetables

Spinach is famous for its high vitamin K content and is a great option for breakfast, paired with an egg and some tomatoes. Use more chili flakes for some extra spice.

Crusty bread

Ingredients (2 servings):

2 eggs

200g tomatoes, chopped

50g spinach

½ teaspoon chili flakes

Prep time: 5 min

Cooking time: 15 min

Preparation:

Heat the oven to 180C/ Gas 6. Wilt the spinach leaves, then squeeze out the excess water and divide between 2 small ovenproof dishes.

Mix the tomatoes with the chili flakes and some optional seasoning then add to the dishes. Make a small well in the center of each dish and crack in an egg. Bake for 15 min and serve.

Nutritional value per serving: 114kcal, 9g protein, 3g carbs (2g fiber, 1g sugar), 7g fat (2g saturated), 0.45g salt, 71% vitamin A, 33% vitamin C, 150% vitamin K, 15% vitamin B2, 21% vitamin B9.

8. Creamy Porridge

Warm up a chilly morning with this healthy creamy porridge. Replace the vanilla extract with some cinnamon to spice things up a bit and give the apple-flavored mix a bit of a spin.

Ingredients (3 servings):

100g porridge oats

100g fresh cranberries

500ml whole milk

1 ½ apple, diced

2 ½ teaspoons granulated brown sugar

½ teaspoon vanilla extract

Prep time: 5 min

Cooking time: 15 min

Preparation:

Cook the apples in a pan with 50ml water until almost softened. Turn up the heat and add the cranberries, half of the sugar and bubble until saucy.

Tip the oats, milk, vanilla and remaining sugar into a saucepan. Bring to a boil while stirring constantly and simmer for 5 min until creamy. Divide between the 3 bowls, top with the fruit mixture and serve.

Nutritional value per serving: 359kcal, 12g protein, 53g carbs (5g fiber, 34g sugar), 9g fat (5g saturated), 0.2g salt, 21% calcium, 16% magnesium, 13% vitamin C, 23% vitamin B1, 22% vitamin B2, 12% vitamin B12.

9. Fruity Muffins

These muffins get their name from a nice blend of fresh and dried fruit and can be frozen for up to 2 weeks without losing any of the flavors. Par them with a cup of almond milk for a 'nuttier' experience.

Ingredients (6 muffins):

110g whole wheat flour

1 large egg

25g butter, melted

90ml skim milk

1 teaspoon baking powder

50 ml clear honey

70g dried apricots, chopped

70g raisins

40g dried cranberries

70g fresh blueberries

½ teaspoon cinnamon

½ teaspoon orange zest, grated

Prep time: 10 min

Cooking time: 25 min

Preparation:

Preheat the oven to 200C fan/ gas 6. Lightly butter a 6-hole muffin tin.

Put the flour and baking powder into a bowl. In another bowl, lightly beat the egg then stir in the melted butter, honey and milk. Add the flour then stir, without turning the mix liquid. Spoon the mixture into the muffin tin and bake for 20-25 min until well risen and golden on the top.

Let them cool for a few minutes then serve.

Nutritional value per muffin: 243kcal, 5g protein, 41g carbs (2g fiber, 10g sugar), 8g fat (3g saturated), 0.6g salt, 13% vitamin A, 11% vitamin B1, 10% vitamin B9.

10. Avocado and Turkey on Toast

You can't miss with a breakfast that contains avocado. Pair the high in healthy fats avocado with a protein-rich turkey and enjoy a meal with a smooth texture and a crunchy slice of ciabatta bread.

Ingredients (2 servings):

1 medium avocado, halved and stoned

2 small slices of ciabatta bread

100g turkey bacon slices

juice from ½ lime

Prep time: 10 min

Cooking time: 5 min

Preparation:

Scrape the avocado flesh into a bowl, squeeze in the lime, season and mash roughly with a fork.

Toast the ciabatta bread, spread the mashed avocado, top with turkey and serve.

Nutritional value per serving: 208kcal, 15g protein, 12g carbs (2g fiber, 1g sugar), 11g fat (2g saturated), 1.3g salt, 16% vitamin C, 10% vitamin E, 26% vitamin K, 13% vitamin B6, 20% vitamin B9.

11. Feta and Semi-dried Tomato Omelette

A really quick, simple, low calorie recipe that is perfect for starting a productive day. For an extra pinch of flavor, use tomatoes that have been preserved in a mixture of olive oil and Italian herbs.

Ingredients (2 servings):

4 eggs, lightly beaten

50g feta cheese, crumbled

8 semi-dried tomatoes, roughly chopped

1 tablespoon olive oil

mixed salad leaves, for serving

Prep time: 5 min

Cooking time: 5 min

Preparation:

Heat the oil in a small, non-stick frying pan, then add the eggs and cook, swirling them with a wooden spoon. When the eggs are a bit runny in the middle, add the tomatoes and feta, then fold the omelette in half. Cook for 1 min then slide it onto a plate. Cut it in half, divide between 2 plates and serve with a mix of leaf salad.

Nutritional value per serving: 300kcal, 18g protein, 20g fat (7 saturated), 5g carbs (1g fiber, 4g sugar), 1.8g salt, 15% calcium, 22% vitamin D, 20% vitamin A, 15% vitamin C, 25% vitamin B12.

LUNCH

12. Rosemary Roasted Chicken Thighs

A high in protein, tasty dish with potatoes that catch the lemony cooking juices and an assortment of ingredients that cover a large spectrum of vitamins and minerals.

Ingredients (2 servings):

4 chicken thighs

250g new potatoes, halved

1 large bunch asparagus, woody ends discarded

½ whole garlic bulb, cloves separated

½ lemon

1 teaspoon olive oil

a small handful rosemary sprigs

a pinch of salt

ground black pepper

Prep time: 10 min

Cooking time: 45min

Preparation:

Heat the oven to 180C fan/ gas 6. Put the potatoes, asparagus, garlic cloves, seasoning (to taste) and oil in a large roasting pan. Squeeze the lemon all over the dish then cut the lemon slices into chunks and toss them in. Mix everything together, cover the dish with foil and roast for about 15 min.

Remove the foil, add the chicken thighs seasoned with a pinch of salt and lots of pepper then roast for another 30 min. When the chicken is crisp and cooked through and the potatoes are tender divide between 2 plates and serve.

Nutritional value per serving: 509kcal, 30g protein, 32g carbs (6g fiber, 5g sugar), 24g fat (6g saturated), 0.3g salt, 14% iron, 14% magnesium, 48% vitamin A, 25% vitamin K, 15% vitamin B1, 15% vitamin B2, 34% vitamin B3, 35% vitamin B6, 12% vitamin B9.

13. Beef Cobbler

An excellent source of B12, this minced beef dish with a low fat and high protein content will keep you satisfied until dinner and also give you the energy you need the entire afternoon.

Ingredients (4 servings):

500g extra-lean beef mince

140g baby chestnut mushrooms, halved

500ml beef stock

1 onion, finely chopped

140g self-rising flour

4 tablespoons low-fat natural yogurt

2 tablespoon plain flour

140g frozen peas

1 tablespoon chopped thyme

a few shakes of Worcestershire sauce

Prep time: 20 min

Cooking time: 50 min

Preparation:

Heat the oven to 160C fan/ gas 4.

Heat a large non-stick frying pan over high heat and dry-fry the minced beef. Stir frequently and cook until browned. Add the mushrooms and the plain flour, then the beef stock and Worchestershire sauce. Bring to a simmer and cook for 10 min.

Mix the self-rising flour and thyme together in a bowl. Stir in the yogurt and enough cold water to form a scone-like dough. Cut the cobbles on a lightly floured surface. The thickness should be of about 1.5cm and the rounds should be about 12x5 cm.

Add the peas to the minced beef mixture then transfer into a baking dish. Place the cobbles on top of the mixture and bake for 25 min until the cobbles are golden brown and risen.

Divide between 4 plates and serve.

Nutritional value per serving: 349kcal, 35g protein, 38g carbs(4g fiber, 5g sugar), 7g fat (3g saturated), 1g salt, 31% iron, 13% magnesium, 15% vitamin A, 11% vitamin C, 12% vitamin K, 38% vitamin B1, 38% vitamin B2, 55% vitamin B3, 30% vitamin B6, 31% vitamin B9, 48% vitamin B12.

14. Salmon and Spinach

High in omega 3 fatty acids and good quality protein, salmon is the perfect fish choice for a main course. Pair with spinach and flavor with a hearty helping of crème fraîche and make yourself the perfect healthy lunch.

Ingredients (2 servings):

2 skinless salmon fillets

250g spinach

2 tablespoons reduced-fat crème fraîche

1 teaspoon caper, drained

1 teaspoon olive oil

juice from ½ lemon

2 tablespoons parsley, chopped

a pinch of sea salt

around black pepper

Prep time: 5 min

Cooking time: 12 min

Preparation:

Heat the oil in a pan, season the salmon with a bit of sea salt and pepper on both sides then fry it for 4 min on each side until the flesh flakes easily. Place it aside on a plate.

Tip the spinach leaves into the hot pan, then cover and let it wilt for 1 min. Spoon the spinach onto the plates, then top with the salmon.

Gently heat the crème fraîche in the pan with a squeeze of lemon juice, the capers and parsley. Be careful not to let it boil. Spoon the sauce over the fish and spinach and serve

Nutritional value per serving: 321kcal, 32g protein, 6g carbs (3g fiber, 3g sugar), 20g fat (5g saturated), 0.8g salt, 14% calcium, 25% iron, 35% magnesium, 239% vitamin A, 58% vitamin C, 20% vitamin E, 756% vitamin K, 24% vitamin B1, 20% vitamin B2, 61% vitamin B3, 26% vitamin B6, 80% vitamin B12.

15. Ratatouille Chicken

A classic chicken recipe that boasts of high quality protein and a mix of vegetables that brings together both flavor and a good amount of vitamins and minerals.

Ingredients (2 servings):

2 skinless chicken breasts

½ small eggplant, cut into chunks

½ zucchini

1 small onion, cut into wedges

2 tomatoes, halved

1 red pepper, cut into chunks

2 tablespoons olive oil, plus extra for drizzling

a few rosemary sprigs

a pinch of salt

ground black pepper

Prep time: 25 min

Cooking time: 35 min

Preparation:

Heat the oven to 200C fan/ gas 6. Lay all the vegetables in a shallow roasting tin. Pour over the olive oil and use your hands to coat all the ingredients.

Put the chicken breasts on top of the vegetables and add the rosemary sprigs. Season everything with the salt and pepper then drizzle a bit of oil over the chicken. Roast for about 35 min then serve.

Nutritional value per serving: 318kcal, 37g protein, 13g crabs (4g fiber), 14g fat (2g saturated), 0.25g salt, 11% iron, 20% magnesium, 60% vitamin A, 177% vitamin C, 20% vitamin E, 33% vitamin K, 16% vitamin B1, 17% vitamin B2, 77% vitamin B3, 57% vitamin B6, 24% vitamin B9.

16. Tuna Salad

Delicious both warm and cold, this tuna salad is a great lunchbox option. With a good helping of vitamin B12, this meal will boost your immune system while bursting with flavor.

Ingredients (4 servings):

160g can tuna in water, drained well

300g new potatoes

175g frozen soya beans

175 green beans, halved

handful of rocket leaves

For the dressing:

2 tablespoons olive oil

1 tablespoon red wine vinegar

2 teaspoons harissa paste

Prep time: 10 min

Cooking time: 15 min

Preparation:

Boil the potatoes until almost tender. Add the beans then cook for another 5 min.

Whisk together the harissa and vinegar in a small bowl with a little seasoning, then whisk in the oil until the dressing has thickened.

Drain the potatoes well, toss in half of the dressing then leave them to cool.

Flake the tuna then fold into the potatoes. Add the remaining dressing and gently toss. Divide between 4 bowls and serve each portion with the rocket leaves.

Nutritional value per serving: 211kcal, 15g protein, 19g carbs (4g fiber, 2g sugar), 9g fat (1g saturated), 0.15g salt, 11% calcium, 25% iron, 30% magnesium, 63% vitamin C, 37% vitamin E, 28% vitamin K, 21% vitamin B1, 18% vitamin B2, 64% vitamin B3, 42% vitamin B6, 72% vitamin B9, 38% vitamin B12.

17. Beef Stew

It might take a while to prepare this delicious stew, but the rich thickness and strong flavor is definitely worth it. You can also make a bigger batch and freeze then defrost it for a no muss, no fuss lunch.

Ingredients (4 servings):

500g stewing beef, cut into large chunks

1 x 400g can chopped tomatoes

1 onion, chopped

200g can butter beans, rinsed and drained

1 teaspoon sweet paprika

1 teaspoon ground cumin

1 teaspoon chili powder

1 tablespoon white/red wine vinegar

1 tablespoon caster sugar

Prep time: 10 min

Cooking time: 3 hours

Preparation:

Heat the oven to 140C fan/ gas 3. Mix the beef, tomatoes, onions, vinegar, sugar and spices in a casserole dish. Cover and bake for 2 ½ hours. Remove the dish from the oven, stir in the beans then bake for another 30 min. Keep the lid off if the casserole is a bit too juicy and on if the consistency is good. Remove from the oven when the beef is tender and serve warm.

Nutritional value per serving: 341kcal, 42g protein, 18g carbs (4g fiber, 11g sugar), 12g fat (5g saturated), 0.95g salt, 23% iron, 14% magnesium, 24% vitamin C, 10% vitamin B1, 11% vitamin B2, 43% vitamin B3, 40% vitamin B6, 22% vitamin B12.

18. Steamed Bass with Cabbage

Bass is another fish that is loaded with omega 3 fatty acids. Coupled with a side of green cabbage that brings lots of vitamins to the mix, this fish a great and flavorful lunch option.

Ingredients (2 servings):

2 sea bass fillets

300g green cabbage, finely shredded

1 red chili, deseeded and finely chopped

2 garlic cloves, thinly sliced

2 teaspoons olive oil

1 teaspoon fresh root ginger

1 teaspoon sesame oil

2 teaspoons low salt soy sauce

a pinch of salt

Prep time: 10 min

Cooking time: 10 min

Preparation:

Sprinkle the fish with the ginger, chili and salt. Steam the cabbage for 5 min then lay the fish on top of the cabbage and steam for another 5 min.

Heat the oils in a small pan, and cook the garlic until lightly browned.

Place the fish and cabbage onto the plates and sprinkle with the soy sauce. Pour over the garlicky oil and serve.

Nutritional value per serving: 188kcal, 23g protein, 11g carbs (4g fiber, 7g sugar), 8g fat (1g saturated), 0.8g salt, 16% magnesium, 92% vitamin C, 147% vitamin K, 15% vitamin B1, 12% vitamin B2, 11% vitamin B3, 35% vitamin B6, 13% vitamin B9.

19. Minestrone

Try this 15 min soup that is high in energy due to its pasta component. The pesto and parmesan topping is both flavorful and colorful and it will keep you coming for more.

Ingredients (2 servings):

500ml hot vegetable stock

50g thin whole wheat spaghetti, broken into short lengths

180g frozen mixed vegetables

200g tin chopped tomatoes

2 tablespoons pesto

vegetarian parmesan-style cheese, coarsely grated, to serve

Prep time: 5 min

Cooking time: 10 min

Preparation:

Bring the stock to a boil with the tomatoes, then add the spaghetti and cook until done. A few minutes before the pasta is ready, add the vegetables and bring back to a boil, then simmer until everything is cooked.

Drizzle with pesto, sprinkle with parmesan and serve.

Nutritional value per serving: 200kcal, 8g protein, 30g carbs (6g fiber, 8g sugar), 5g fat, 0.55g salt, 12% iron, 11% magnesium, 81% vitamin A, 18% vitamin C.

20. Chicken Salad

This simple chicken salad is a good example of a quick lunch that can be packed and taken to go. The blend of greens, chicken, fish oil and sugar makes for an intriguing palette.

Ingredients (2 servings):

2 skinless chicken breasts

½ red onion, thinly sliced,

½ cucumber, sliced

200g mixed salad leaves

2 tablespoons fish sauce

1 tablespoon caster sugar

1 chili pepper, deseeded and thinly sliced

zest and juice from 1 lime

large handful of coriander, roughly chopped

Prep time: 10 min

Cooking time: 15 min

Preparation:

Cover the chicken with cold water, bring to a boil and cook for 10 min. When the chicken is done, tear it into shreds.

Stir together the fish sauce, sugar, lime juice and zest until the sugar dissolves.

Divide the leaves and coriander between plates, top with the chicken, onion, chili pepper and cucumber then toss through with the dressing and serve.

Nutritional value per serving: 218kcal, 38g protein, 12g carbs (10g fiber, 3g sugar), 2g fat, 11% iron, 14% magnesium, 149% vitamin A, 39% vitamin C, 232% vitamin K, 12% vitamin B1, 12% vitamin B2, 68% vitamin B3, 38% vitamin B6, 13% vitamin B9.

21. Spaghetti with Sardines

Sardines are both delicious and high in vitamin B12. Combined with spaghetti and topped with a garlicky tomato sauce they create a nice balance of vitamins, protein and energy-infusing carbs.

Ingredients (2 servings):

200g whole wheat spaghetti

95g can skinless and boneless sardines in tomato sauce

1 x 100g can chopped tomatoes

50g pitted black olives, roughly chopped

1 clove garlic, crushed

1 teaspoon capers, drained

1 teaspoon olive oil

a pinch of chili flakes

a small handful parsley, chopped

Prep time: 5 min

Cooking time: 15 min

Preparation:

Cook the spaghetti according to the instructions on the pack.

Heat the oil in a pan and cook the garlic for 1 min. Add the sardines, tomatoes, chili flakes, breaking roughly with a spoon. Heat for 2-3 min then stir in the capers, olives and most of the parsley. Mix well.

Drain the pasta, reserving a few tablespoons of water. Add the pasta to the sauce, mix well then pour in the reserved water if the sauce is a little thick. Divide between 2 bowls, sprinkle with the rest of the parsley and serve.

Nutritional value per serving: 495kcal, 21g protein, 77g carbs (5g fiber, 5g sugar), 14g fat (2g saturated), 1.1g salt, 15% calcium, 18% iron, 18% magnesium, 58% vitamin D, 12% vitamin B2, 21% vitamin B3, 10% vitamin B6, 70% vitamin B12.

22.   Chicken Curry with Peanut Butter

This chicken curry is rich in vitamin B3 and high quality protein. Serve it with a side of steamed brown rice that goes well with the peanut butter sauce and brings carbs to the table if needed.

Ingredients (2 servings):

2 skinless chicken breasts, cut into chunks

100g Greek Yogurt

75ml chicken stock

2 ½ tablespoons peanut butter

1 small red chili pepper, deseeded

1 small garlic clove

¼ of a finger-length fresh root ginger, roughly chopped

1 teaspoon olive oil

a small bunch of coriander, stalks roughly chopped

Prep time: 5 min

Cooking time: 15 min

Preparation:

Finely slice a quarter of the chili pepper then put the rest in a food processor with the garlic, coriander stalk, 1/3 of the leaves and ginger. Make a rough paste and add a splash of water if needed.

Heat the oil in a pan and quickly brown the chicken for 1 min. Stir in the paste for 1 min then add the yogurt, stock and peanut butter. Cook for another 10 min until the sauce has thickened and the chicken is cooked through.

Nutritional value per serving: 358kcal, 43g protein, 4g carbs (1g fiber, 3g sugar), 19g fat (6g saturated), 0.7g salt, 14% magnesium, 76% vitamin B3, 36% vitamin B6.

23. Salmon and Brown Rice Salad

A zesty recipe that has the ideal combination of lean protein, heart-healthy fats and slow-releasing carbs. The salmon and brown rice salad is high in vitamins and has an oriental soy-based flavor.

Ingredients (2 servings):

1 salmon fillet, skinless

100g brown basmati rice

100g frozen soya beans, defrosted

2 teaspoons low sodium soy sauce

1 cucumber, diced

½ red chili, diced

zest and juice from ½ lime

a small bunch of spring onions, sliced

a small bunch of coriander, roughly chopped

Prep time: 15 min

Cooking time: 25 min

Preparation:

Cook the rice following the instructions on the pack, and 3 min before it's done, add the soya beans. Drain and cool under cold running water.

Put the salmon on a plate, and microwave it on high until cooked through (about 3 min). Flake the salmon then gently, fold it with the spring onions, cucumber, coriander, rice and beans.

Mix the lime juice and zest, soy and chili in a separate bowl, pour over the rice dish and serve.

Nutritional value per serving: 497kcal, 34g protein, 61g carbs (5g fiber, 6 g sugar), 15g fat (3g saturated), 1.5g salt, 10% calcium, 19% iron, 31% magnesium, 14% vitamin A, 24% vitamin C, 146% vitamin K, 32% vitamin B1, 16% vitamin B2, 63% vitamin B3, 22% vitamin B6, 49% vitamin B9, 80% vitamin B12.

DINNER

24. Lentil Dhal with Eggplant

A high fiber and vitamins dinner, the lentil Dahl with grilled eggplant is an original way to combine a simple assortment of vegetables flavored with Indian spices.

Ingredients (2 servings):

100g lentils, rinsed

1 medium eggplant, cut into slices (2 cm)

1 medium onion, thinly sliced

1 garlic clove, finely chopped

3 cm piece of ginger, grated

1 tablespoon tamarind paste

2 tablespoons olive oil

1 teaspoon turmeric

1 teaspoon curry powder

¼ teaspoon salt

a pinch of ground black pepper

Prep time: 10 min

Cooking time: 25 min

Preparation:

Pour 500 ml water over the lentils, tamarind paste and turmeric. Add some of the salt and boil until very soft, making sure to skim off any foam that forms on the top.

Heat 1 tablespoon of the oil and cook the onion, ginger and garlic until golden. Add the curry powder and cook for another 2 min. Pour in the lentil mixture and cook for 10 min.

Heat a griddle pan until very hot. Rub 1 tablespoon of oil over the eggplant slices and season with the black pepper and the rest of the salt. Cook for 2 min on each side until charred.

Place the lentil mix on a plate, top with the grilled eggplant slices and serve.

Nutritional value per serving: 325kcal 15g protein, 41g carbs (7g fiber, 10g sugar), 13g fat (1g saturated), 0.75g salt, 24% iron, 25% magnesium, 14% vitamin E, 23% vitamin K, 36% Vitamin B1, 12% vitamin B2, 14% vitamin B3, 26% vitamin B6, 75% vitamin B9.

25. Spicy Spaghetti

An easy to make, low fat meal that is high in nutrients and loaded with vegetables. For an extra spicy taste, don't deseed the red chili and enjoy the hotness.

Ingredients (4 servings):

300g whole wheat spaghetti

250g chestnut mushrooms, thinly sliced

1 x 400g can chopped tomatoes

1 garlic clove, thinly sliced

1 medium onion, finely chopped

1 celery stick, finely chopped

½ red chili, deseeded and finely chopped

2 tablespoons olive oil

a small bunch of parsley, leaves only, chopped

a pinch of salt

Prep time: 10 min

Cooking time: 15 min

Preparation:

Cook the spaghetti according to the instructions on the pack, then drain.

Heat 1 tablespoon of oil in a pan, add the mushrooms and fry for 3 min until softened. Add the garlic, fry for 1 more min then tip the mix in a bowl with the parsley.

Heat the rest of the oil, add the celery and onion and cook for 5 min. Stir in the tomatoes, chili and a little salt. Bring to a boil, reduce the heat and simmer for 10 min, uncovered, until the sauce has thickened.

Toss the spaghetti with the sauce, top with the mushrooms and serve.

Nutritional value per serving: 346kcal, 12g protein, 62g carbs (5g fiber, 7g sugar), 7g fat (1g saturated), 0.35g salt, 22% iron, 15% magnesium, 19% vitamin C, 10% vitamin E, 12% vitamin K, 51% vitamin B1, 33% vitamin B2, 40% vitamin B3, 11% vitamin B6, 49% vitamin B9.

26. Spinach and Tofu Cannelloni

This tasty tofu and spinach meal is a vegetarian's best friend. Packed with vitamins and minerals, this dish is both delicious and healthy and it has the added value of tasting very well after being frozen.

Ingredients (6 servings):

300g lasagna sheets

350g silken tofu

400g spinach

2 x 400g cans chopped tomatoes

3 garlic cloves, finely chopped

1 large onion, chopped

50g pine nuts, chopped

4 tablespoons fresh breadcrumbs

2 tablespoons olive oil

a pinch of grated nutmeg

pepper, to taste

Prep time: 25 min

Cooking time: 1 h

Preparation:

Heat the olive oil in a pan, add the onion and 1/3 of the garlic and fry until softened. Pour in the tomatoes, season and bring to a boil, then reduce the heat and cook for 10 min until the sauce has thickened.

Heat the remaining oil and cook another 1/3 of the garlic for 1 min, add the spinach and pine nuts. Cook until the spinach has wilted then tip out the excess liquid.

Blend the tofu with a hand blender until smooth then mix with the spinach, nutmeg and some pepper. Remove from heat and allow it to cool slightly.

Heat the oven to 200 fan/ gas 6. Pour half the tomato sauce into an ovenproof dish. Spread the lasagna sheets on a plate, divide the spinach amongst them then roll them up and place over the sauce. Pour over the remaining sauce and bake for 30 min.

Mix the crumbs with the rest of the garlic and pine nuts, sprinkle them over the top of the dish, drizzle with the remaining oil and bake for 10 min until the crumbs are golden. Serve warm.

Nutritional value per serving: 284kcal, 13g protein, 30g carbs (4g fiber, 6g sugar), 13g fat (2g saturated), 0.65g salt, 25% calcium, 30% iron, 29% magnesium, 129% vitamin A, 52% vitamin C, 19% vitamin E, 417% vitamin K, 15% vitamin B1, 16% vitamin B2, 13% vitamin B3, 13% vitamin B6, 41% vitamin B9.

27. Green Bean and Corn Cakes

Try these vegetarian fritters made with spring onions, beans and sweet corn. Serve them with a side of creamy lime avocado and sweet dipping sauce and delight your taste buds.

Ingredients (2 servings):

1 x 200g sweet corn kernels, boiled and drained

25g green beans, chopped

50g self-rising flour

1 small avocado, diced

125g Tracklemans chili jam

½ red chili, deseeded, finely chopped

1 large egg, beaten

2 spring onions, chopped

40ml milk

juice from ½ lime

1 tablespoon olive oil

a small handful of coriander leaves

a pinch of salt

a pinch of ground black pepper

Prep time: 10 min

Cooking time: 10 min

Preparation:

Mix together the eggs, milk, sweet corn, spring onions, beans, flour, milk, half the chili, half the coriander and some seasoning in a large bowl. Mix the avocado with the rest of the coriander, chili and lime juice.

Heat the olive oil in a non-stick frying pan and spoon in 3 mounds of the corn mixture, a little spaced apart. When browned on one side, turn over and cook for another 2 min. Repeat with the remaining batter. Serve the cakes warm with the avocado salsa and chili jam.

Nutritional value per serving: 353kcal, 9g protein, 35g carbs (5g fiber, 8g sugar), 20g fat (4g saturated, 0.8g salt, 13% iron, 17% vitamin C, 21% vitamin K, 18% vitamin B1, 16% vitamin B2, 16% vitamin B3, 13% vitamin B6, 38% vitamin B9.

28. Rosemary Risotto

Give an interesting spin to a risotto recipe by adding artichokes, toasted pine nuts and a hearty helping of rosemary needles and enjoy a richly-flavored dinner.

Ingredients (2 servings):

70g Arborio risotto rice

200g tin artichoke hearts in water, drained and halved

1 red onion, sliced into thin wedges

1 red pepper, cut into chunks

75ml white wine

400ml low-salt vegetable stock

1 tablespoon toasted pine nuts

1 tablespoon grated parmesan

1 teaspoon olive oil

1 tablespoon rosemary needles

a pinch of salt

Prep time: 15 min

Cooking time: 35 min

Preparation:

Heat the oil in a wok. Cook the onions on medium heat for 6-7 min until softened and browning. Add the peppers and rosemary and cook for another 5 min. Throw in the rice and stir. Pour in the wine and half of the stock, bring to a boil, then reduce the heat and simmer gently until almost all of the liquid is absorbed. Stir in the rest of the stock and proceed as described above. Add the artichokes and simmer again until the rice is tender.

Season with a pinch of salt, stir in the Parmesan cheese and ½ of the pine nuts. Scatter over the remaining pine nuts and serve.

Nutritional value per serving: 299kcal, 9g protein, 44g carbs (4g fiber, 9g sugar), 10g fat (2g saturated), 0.7g salt, 18% magnesium, 86% vitamin C, 11% vitamin K, 15% vitamin B1, 12% vitamin B3, 20% vitamin B6.

29. Pear and Blue Cheese Salad

Grill juicy pears and contrast the sweet taste with a robust blue cheese and honey vinaigrette in this intriguing salad mix. Add a handful of rocket leaves for more greens and vitamins.

Ingredients (2 servings):

2 firm, ripe pears, sliced lengthways into 1 cm slices

75g blue cheese, crumbled

1 tablespoon olive oil

1 teaspoon honey

1 teaspoon white wine vinegar

120g mixed salad leaves

Prep time: 10 min

Cooking time: 15 min

Preparation:

Drizzle the pears with a bit of the oil. Heat a griddle pan, cook the pears for 1 min on each side, then set aside to cool.

Mix the rest of the oil, the honey and vinegar. Toss the pears with the cheese and leaves, then divide between 2 plates, drizzle with the dressing and serve.

Nutritional value per serving: 259kcal, 8g protein, 24g carbs (5g fiber, 19g sugar), 17g fat (8g saturated), 1.2g salt, 20% calcium, 13% vitamin A, 14% vitamin C, 31% vitamin K, 11% vitamin B2, 11% vitamin B9.

30. Baked Polenta

This Italian mineral and vitamin fest is both nutritious and delicious. Customize this dish according to taste by combining the goat's cheese with blue cheese/parmesan cheese/Cheshire cheese.

Ingredients (4 servings):

500g pack ready-made polenta

2 x 400g cans chopped tomatoes

100g goat's cheese with rind, broken into chunks

300g fresh spinach

3 garlic cloves, chopped

1 tablespoon olive oil

a pinch of salt

Prep time: 20 min

Cooking time: 20 min

Preparation:

Heat the oven to 220C fan/ gas 7 and boil the kettle. In a bowl, mix the tomatoes with the garlic and salt, then pour into a large baking dish. Wilt the spinach, then rinse in cold water and squeeze out all off the excess liquid. Roughly chop the spinach and scatter on top of the tomatoes.

Slice the polenta then place the pieces on top of the spinach. Drizzle with the oil and bake for about 15 min. Scatter over the cheese then return to the over for 5 more min. Serve hot.

Nutritional value per serving: 240kcal, 12g protein, 26g carbs (6g fiber, 7g sugar), 10g fat (5g saturated), 1.6g salt, 25% calcium, 110% iron, 23% magnesium, 169% vitamin A, 61% vitamin C, 18% vitamin E, 462% vitamin K, 11% vitamin B1, 28% vitamin B2, 12% vitamin B3, 1-% vitamin B6, 39% vitamin B9.

31. Vegetable Tagine

Healthy and filling, this vegetarian dish makes use of chickpeas, zucchini and peas in a mix that is topped by a daring combination of spices and a sweet serving of raisins.

Ingredients (2 servings):

200g can chickpeas, rinsed and drained

1 large zucchini, cut into chunks

1 onion, chopped

1 tomato, chopped

150g frozen peas

200ml vegetable stock

2 tablespoons raisins

1 tablespoon olive oil

¼ teaspoon ground cinnamon

¼ teaspoon ground coriander

¼ teaspoon ground cumin

chopped coriander, to serve

Prep time: 10 min

Cooking time: 20 min

Preparation:

Heat the oil in a pan, then fry the onions for 5 min until soft. Add the spices, tomato, zucchini, chickpeas, raisins and stock and bring to a boil. Cover and simmer for 10 min then stir in the peas and cook for 5 more min. Sprinkle with coriander and serve.

Nutritional value per serving: 246kcal, 12g protein, 36g carbs (9g fiber, 19g sugar), 9g fat (1g saturated), 0.55g salt, 13% iron, 21% magnesium, 44% vitamin K, 25% vitamin B1, 22% vitamin B2, 13% vitamin B3, 52% vitamin B6, 45% vitamin B9.

32. Spiced Quinoa

Quinoa is a good source of vegetable protein and is nicely flavored by feta cheese and toasted flaked almonds. Enjoy the lemon-flavored zesty dish and the hearty amount of magnesium and vitamins.

Ingredients (2 servings):

150g quinoa, rinsed

50g feta cheese, crumbled

25g toasted flaked almonds

juice form ¼ lemon

¼ teaspoon turmeric

½ teaspoon ground coriander

1 teaspoon olive oil

a handful of parsley, roughly chopped

Prep time: 10 min

Cooking time: 15 min

Preparation:

Heat the oil in a large pan, then add the spices and fry until fragrant. Add the quinoa, and fry for another min until you can hear popping sounds. Stir in 300 ml boiling water then gently simmer for about 10 min until the water has evaporated and the grains have a white halo around them. Allow to cool slightly then stir through the other ingredients and serve.

Nutritional value per serving: 404kcal, 17g protein, 44g carbs (1g fiber, 6 g sugar), 19g fat (4g saturated), 0.7g salt, 15% calcium, 19% iron, 37% magnesium, 11% vitamin E, 20% vitamin B1, 37% vitamin B2, 23% vitamin B6, 36% vitamin B9.

33. Vegetable Pie

Try this vitamin A loaded pie that brings a high variety of vegetables to the table. The mashed potatoes crust is ingenious while the filling is a delight to taste.

Ingredients (4 servings):

900g potatoes, cut into chunks

200g frozen peas

½ cauliflower, broken into small florets

300g carrots, cut into small batons

1 x 400g can chopped tomatoes

4 garlic cloves, finely sliced

2 onions, sliced

200ml milk

1 rosemary sprig, leaves finely chopped

1 teaspoon flour

1 tablespoon olive oil

a pinch of salt

Prep time: 15 min

Cooking time: 45 min

Preparation:

Heat 1 teaspoon of the oil in a flameproof dish over medium heat. Add the onions and cook until softened, then stir in the flour and cook for another 2 min. Add the cauliflower, carrots, garlic and rosemary and cook for 5 min, stirring regularly.

Tip in the tomatoes and a cup full of water. Cover with a lid and simmer for 10 min, then remove the lid and cook for another 10 min until the sauce has thickened and the vegetables are cooked. Season, stir in the peas and cook for 1 min.

Boil the potatoes, drain and mash them. Stir through enough milk to reach a soft consistency then add the remaining olive oil.

Heat the grill, spoon the vegetable mix (hot) into a pie dish, top with the mashed potatoes and place under the grill for a few minutes until the top is golden brown. Serve hot.

Nutritional value per serving: 388kcal, 15g protein, 62g carbs (11g fiber, 18g sugar), 8g fat (2g saturated), 0.3g salt, 17% calcium, 24% iron, 47% magnesium, 263% vitamin A, 51% vitamin K, 32% vitamin B1, 21% vitamin B2, 25% vitamin B3, 55% vitamin B6, 34% vitamin B9.

34. Squash and Lentil Salad

This vibrant salad makes use of canned lentils and juicy butternut squash. The result is a high-fiber salad that contains more than a day's worth of vitamin A, K and B9.

Ingredients (2 servings):

500g butternut squash, cut into chunks

1 x 400g can Puy lentils in water, drained

50g spinach

70g cherry tomatoes, halved

1 garlic clove, crushed

¼ red onion, sliced

20g Cheshire cheese, crumbled

1 teaspoon thyme leaves

1 teaspoon balsamic vinegar

½ teaspoon wholegrain mustard

1 tablespoon toasted pumpkin seeds

1 teaspoon olive oil

a pinch of salt

Prep time: 10 min

Cooking time: 30 min

Preparation:

Heat the oven to 180C fan/ gas 4. Toss the squash with half of the olive oil, garlic clove, seasoning and thyme leaves in a baking dish and roast for 25 min or until tender.

Mix together the vinegar, mustard, 1 tablespoon of water and the rest of the olive oil. Toss the lentils with the dressing, onion, cherry tomatoes and spinach.

Divide the lentil between two plates, then top with the squash, Cheshire cheese and pumpkin seeds then serve.

Nutritional value per serving: 304kcal, 15g protein, 41g carbs (13g fiber, 15g sugar), 10g fat (3g saturated), 0.35g salt, 17% calcium, 67% iron, 42% magnesium, 610% vitamin A, 88% vitamin C, 24% vitamin E, 166% vitamin K, 27% vitamin B1, 24% vitamin B2, 14% vitamin B3, 35% vitamin B6, 119% vitamin B9.

35. Grapefruit Salad

Load yourself with vitamin A and C with a grapefruit based salad that is sweetened by agave nectar. This quickly-made, pistachio-flavored salad will leave you satisfied and refreshed.

Ingredients (2 servings):

1 medium pink grapefruit

1 medium white grapefruit

1 teaspoon pistachio, chopped

1 tablespoon agave nectar

Prep time: 5 min

No cooking

Preparation:

Segment the grapefruits, removing as much of the pith as possible. Divide the segments between two bowls, top with the pistachios and agave nectar and serve.

Nutritional value per serving: 107kcal, 2g protein, 21g carbs (2g fiber, 12g sugar), 1g fat, 56% vitamin A, 128% vitamin C.

SNACKS

1. Apple Crisps

Core 2 Granny Smith apples and slice through the equator then place them on a baking sheet, sprinkle with cinnamon and bake for 45 min.

Nutritional value: 90kcal, 25g carbs (3g fiber, 22g sugar), 14% vitamin C.

2. Dried Apricot Bar

Pureé 140g apricots with 150ml boiling water and 40g oats in a food processor. Toast 40g desiccated coconut with 25g sunflower seeds and 1 tablespoon sesame seeds in a non-stick pan over low heat, then stir in the apricots with 15g dried cranberries, 3 tablespoons hemp protein powder and 1 tablespoon chia seeds. Make a thick paste then roll it onto a long sheet of cling film and wrap tightly. Chill then cut into 14 slices.

Nutritional value per slice: 78kcal, 3g protein, 8g carbs (3g fiber, 5g sugar), 4g fat (2g saturated),

3. Avocado on Toast

Toast a small piece of whole wheat bread then cover it with 50g of mashed avocado and sprinkle with salt and pepper.

Nutritional value: 208kcal, 5g protein, 28g carbs (6g fiber, 2g sugar), 9g fat (1g saturated), 0.5g salt, 13% vitamin K, 13% vitamin B9.

4. Smoothie

In a blender, mix ½ cup blueberries, 1 cup spinach leaves, ½ cup low-fat Greek Yogurt and ½ cup pineapple coconut water.

Nutritional value: 168kcal, 24g carbs (3g fiber, 8g sugar), 17g protein, 23% calcium, 57% vitamin A, 73% vitamin C, 199% vitamin K, 16% vitamin B9.

5. Trail Mix

Mix together 10g walnuts, 10g almond and 30g raisins.

Nutritional value: 217kcal, 4g protein, 25g carbs (2g fiber, 17g sugar), 13g fat (1g saturated), 10% magnesium.

6. Energy Nuggets

Blend 50g dried apricots and 50g dried cherries in a food processor until very finely chopped. Tip into a bowl and mix with 2 teaspoons coconut oil. Shape the mix into walnut-sized balls then roll in 1 tablespoon toasted sesame seeds. Makes 6 nuggets.

Nutritional value per nugget: 113kcal, 2g protein, 21g carbs (2g fiber, 18g sugar), 3g fat (1g saturated).

7. Blueberry Yogurt

Blend 150g low fat yogurt with ½ cup blueberries.

Nutritional value: 136kcal, 8g protein, 21g carbs (2g fiber, 18g sugar), 3g fat (1g saturated), 27% calcium, 13% vitamin C, 18% vitamin K, 21% vitamin B2, 13% vitamin B12.

8. Cup of Popcorn

Nutritional value: 31kcal, 1g protein, 6g carbs (1g fiber).

9. Apple and Peanut Butter

Slice 1 small apple and spread 1 tablespoon creamy peanut butter on the pieces.

Nutritional value: 189kcal, 4g protein, 28g carbs (5g fiber, 20g sugar), 8g fat (1g saturated), 14% vitamin C, 14% vitamin B3.

10. Roasted Chickpeas

Nutritional value 50g: 96kcal, 4g protein, 13g carbs (4g fiber, 2g sugar), 3g fat.

11. Strawberry Greek Yogurt

Mix 150g Greek Yogurt with 5 medium-sized strawberries cut in half.

Nutritional value: 150kcal, 11g protein, 10g carbs (10g sugar), 8g fat (5g saturated), 10% calcium, 60% vitamin C.

12. Cinnamon Oranges

Remove the rind and pith from an orange then cut it into slices and add 1 teaspoon of orange juice, 1 teaspoon of lemon juice, ¼ teaspoon of sugar and a dash of cinnamon.

Nutritional value per serving: 86kcal, 1g protein, 22g carbs (3g fiber, 19g sugar), 116% vitamin C, 10% vitamin B9.

13. Grilled Asparagus

Cook 100g asparagus in boiling water for 2 min. Drain then toss with a little olive oil. Grill the asparagus spears for a few minutes then drizzle with a knob of melted butter and 1 teaspoon of toasted flaked almonds.

Nutritional value: 107kcal, 4g protein, 4g carbs (2g fiber, 2 g sugar), 9g fat (3g saturated), 0.1g salt, 12% iron, 15% vitamin A, 52% vitamin K, 10% vitamin B1, 13% vitamin B9.

14. Soya Milk Smoothie

Blend ½ banana with 125ml soya milk, ½ teaspoon honey and a little grated nutmeg until smooth. Top with 1 teaspoon chopped hazelnuts.

Nutritional value per serving: 220kcal, 8g protein, 24g carbs (1g fiber, 21g sugar), 10g fat (1g saturated), 0.2g salt, 14% vitamin B2, 11% vitamin B6.

JUICE RECIPES TO LOWER YOUR BLOOD PRESSURE

1. Surprise Sunrise

This juice recipe is a problem solver when it comes to issues with high blood pressure. It's rich in vitamins and minerals that will turn your body into a healthy energy factory.

Benefits:

Celery is well known for having a high calcium content. Celery helps controlling high blood pressure. Pears have anti-oxidants which help prevent high blood pressure.

Ingredients:

- Apples - 2 medium 360g
- Carrots - 2 medium 122g
- Celery - 3 stalk, large 190g
- Lemons (peeled) - 2 fruit 165g
- Pears - 2 medium 356g

How to prepare:

- **Wash all the ingredients thoroughly.**
- **Juice them well and enjoy this fresh drink right away.**

Total calories: 381

Vitamins: Vitamin A 785ug, Vitamin C 187mg, Calcium 130mg

Minerals: Sodium 221mg, Potassium 2454mg

Sugars 55g

2. Light Cream

The best way to keep you relaxed and full of energy during the day is to start with a natural juice. Here is a great recipe that will do more than that, check it out.

Benefits:

Certain protein compounds that you find only in spinach are great to lower high blood pressure. Bell pepper is known to reduce cholesterol and high blood pressure.

Ingredients:

- Cucumber - 1/2 cucumber 150g
- Parsley - 2 handful 80g
- Pepper - 1/2 medium 59g
- Spinach - 1 cup 30g
- Tomatoes - 3 medium whole 350g
- Cabbage (red) - 1 leaf 22g

How to prepare:

- **Wash all the ingredients thoroughly.**
- **Juice them well and enjoy this fresh drink right away.**

Total calories: 115

Vitamins: Vitamin A 205ug, Vitamin C 97mg, Calcium 221mg

Minerals: Sodium 212mg, Potassium 1755mg

Sugars 13g

3. Mind Lifting

A variety of fruits and vegetables make this a great to have a healthy body. That's why this recipe is a powerful and healthy one, and you should try it in the morning.

Benefits:

A recent study has shown that foods high in potassium lower blood pressure as well. Oranges are a great source of vitamin C.

Ingredients:

- Cucumber - 1 cucumber 300g
- Oranges - 2 fruit 260g
- Pineapple - 1/4 fruit 226.25g
- Spinach - 5 handful 125g
- Banana – 1 medium 90g

How to prepare:

- **Wash all the ingredients thoroughly.**
- **Juice them well and enjoy this fresh drink right away.**

Total calories: 184

Vitamins: Vitamin A 421ug, Vitamin C 154mg, Calcium 202mg

Minerals: Sodium 71mg, Potassium 1322mg

Sugars 30g

4. HT Juice

When you want a healthy body and mind you should add different juice recipes that include leafy vegetables and mixing them with better tasting ingredients to improve the flavor of the drink.

Benefits:

Lime juice is helpful for people that suffer heart problems because it contains potassium. It also helps to control blood pressure, and reduces mental stress.

Ingredients:

- Apples - 2 medium 364g
- Kale - 5 leaf 175g
- Lime - 1/2 fruit 32g
- Orange - 150g
- Carrots -1 large 70g

How to prepare:

- **Wash all the ingredients thoroughly.**
- **Juice them well and enjoy this fresh drink right away.**

Total calories: 160

Vitamins: Vitamin A 300ug, Vitamin C 191mg, Calcium 109mg

Minerals: Sodium 103mg, Potassium 1437mg

Sugars 43g

5. Big A

You can always use a new juice recipe that contains all essential minerals and vitamins that will lead your body in the end to a healthier one. This is another great morning drink.

Benefits:

Pectin in apples lowers cholesterol levels and can also help lower blood pressure. Pear juice has an anti-inflammatory effect and is a very good nutrient provider.

Ingredients:

- Apples - 2 medium 360g
- Orange (peeled) - 1 fruit 130g
- Pears - 2 medium 356g
- Sweet Potato - 130g
- Lime ½ - 33g

How to prepare:

- **Wash all the ingredients thoroughly.**
- **Juice them well and enjoy this fresh drink right away.**

Total calories: 307

Vitamins: Vitamin A 610ug, Vitamin C 61mg, Calcium 123mg

Minerals: Sodium 120mg, Potassium 1221mg

Sugars 60g

6. Sweet Day

This juice recipe is a great one if you want a positive change in your heart. If you have had heart problems in the past try this drink and see what it may do for you.

Benefits:

Beets have medicinal properties, they help normalize blood pressure, and they also are high in carbohydrates, a great source of instant energy.

Ingredients:

- Beet Root (golden) - 1 beet 80g
- Carrots - 3 large 215g
- Cucumber - 1/2 cucumber 150g
- Ginger Root - 1/2 thumb 12g
- Lime- ½ 33g

How to prepare:

- **Wash all the ingredients thoroughly.**
- **Juice them well and enjoy this fresh drink right away.**

Total calories: 137

Vitamins: Vitamin A 1104ug, Vitamin C 19mg, Calcium 143mg

Minerals: Sodium 265mg, Potassium 1391mg

Sugars 22g

7. Green God

You should try this juice recipe at lunch because it's very rich in nutrients that will be better absorbed during that time of the day and be easier for you to digest.

Benefits:

Cucumber is an essential component of healthy connective tissue, and it also helps lower blood pressure.

Ingredients:

- Celery - 4 stalk, large 255g
- Cucumber - 1 cucumber 300g
- Ginger Root - 1 thumb 24g
- Lemon - 1/2 fruit 42g

How to prepare:

- **Wash all the ingredients thoroughly.**
- **Juice them well and enjoy this fresh drink right away.**

Total calories: 183

Vitamins: Vitamin A 764ug, Vitamin C 171mg, Calcium 312mg

Minerals: Sodium 195mg, Potassium 1872mg

Sugars 30g

8. Healing Mix

Here is another great juice recipe that will help you improve your health and the way you feel. If the combination of lemon and orange is too strong for you, simply eliminate one of the two but if you can drink them together it will be better.

Benefits:

Lemon juice reduces depression and controls high blood pressure, and consuming vitamin C helps to lower the incidence of peptic ulcers.

Ingredients:

- Celery - 4 stalk, large 255g
- Lemon (with rind) - 1/2 fruit 28g
- Orange (peeled) - 1 large 180g
- Spinach - 5 handful 125g

How to prepare:

- **Wash all the ingredients thoroughly.**
- **Juice them well and enjoy this fresh drink right away.**

Total calories: 202

Vitamins: Vitamin A 250ug, Vitamin C 87mg, Calcium 211mg

Minerals: Sodium 211mg, Potassium 1501mg

Sugars 40g

9. GROWL Juice

Juice recipes are a fast way to keep up with a modern lifestyle for individuals that are looking to have a healthy body. This is a great recipe to lower blood pressure and strengthen your heart.

Benefits:

Ginger might have a role in lowering cholesterol and also helps lower high blood pressure. The extract from apple skin may lower risk of liver cancer so it would be better if you wash well and include the skin when juicing.

Ingredients:

- Apples - 2 medium 365g
- Celery - 3 stalk, large 192g
- Cucumber - 1 cucumber 300g
- Lime (with rind) - 1 fruit 65g
- Parsley - 1 bunch 150g

How to prepare:

- **Wash all the ingredients thoroughly.**
- **Juice them well and enjoy this fresh drink right away.**

Total calories: 202

Vitamins: Vitamin A 590ug, Vitamin C 156mg, Calcium 281mg

Minerals: Sodium 197mg, Potassium 1789mg

Sugars 28g

10. All Star Juice

Start your day strong with this great mix of fruits and delicious vegetables. These ingredients are perfect for you because they are rich in nutrients and vitamins.

Benefits:

Pears contain anti-carcinogen glutathione that helps prevent blood pressure. Carrots are rich in beta-carotene and they also may reduce high blood pressure.

Ingredients:

- Carrots - 4 medium 220g
- Cucumber - 1 cucumber 300g
- Lemon - 1 fruit 58g
- Pear - 1 medium 178g
- Celery - 1 stalk, large 62g

How to prepare:

- **Wash all the ingredients thoroughly.**
- **Juice them well and enjoy this fresh drink right away.**

Total calories: 210

Vitamins: Vitamin A 1044ug, Vitamin C 40mg, Calcium 139mg

Minerals: Sodium 149mg, Potassium 1451mg

Sugars 32g

11. Junior Juice

When each second is precious and you feel like you are running out of time to get healthier, you should not neglect your body, that is why this awesome juice recipe will do wonders for you and your body in a very short period of time.

Benefits:

Celery is great for lowering high blood pressure and it's a great source of nutrients.

Ingredients:

- Celery - 3 stalk, large 190g
- Cucumber - 1/2 cucumber 150g
- Ginger Root - 1/2 thumb 12g
- Kale - 2 leaf 70g
- Banana - 1 medium 90g

How to prepare:

- **Wash all the ingredients thoroughly.**
- **Juice them well and enjoy this fresh drink right away.**

Total calories: 200

Vitamins: Vitamin A 503ug, Vitamin C 176mg, Calcium 276mg

Minerals: Sodium 133mg, Potassium 1569mg

Sugars 45g

12. Mr. Heart Healthy Mix

Make sure you start your day with this heart healthy mix with a great flavor thanks to the banana and apple combination.

Benefits:

Bananas play an important role in reducing blood pressure. Apples lower cholesterol and also increase bone density.

Ingredients:

- Carrots - 4 medium 242g
- Celery - 3 stalk, large 190g
- Ginger Root - 1/2 thumb 11g
- Banana – 1 medium 90g
- Apple – 1 medium 180g

How to prepare:

- **Wash all the ingredients thoroughly.**
- **Juice them well and enjoy this fresh drink right away.**

Total calories: 233

Vitamins: Vitamin A 1312ug, Vitamin C 27mg, Calcium 143mg

Minerals: Sodium 310mg, Potassium 1670mg

Sugars 44g

13. Sunny Start Breakfast Drink

Here is a great juice recipe that you can start your day with. It will keep your energy levels high during the entire day and will also be an excellent source of vitamins, so check it out.

Benefits:

Tomatoes have been known to be excellent for your heart and may lower their blood pressure. They are also a great source of vitamin C.

Ingredients:

- Apples (green) - 1 medium 180g
- Cucumber - 1 cucumber 300g
- Grapes (green) - 15 grape 90g
- Spinach - 2 cup 60g
- Tomato - 1 medium whole 121g

How to prepare:

- **Wash all the ingredients thoroughly.**
- **Juice them well and enjoy this fresh drink right away.**

Total calories: 179

Vitamins: Vitamin A 540ug, Vitamin C 59mg, Calcium 144mg

Minerals: Sodium 112mg, Potassium 1448mg

Sugars 31g

14. Beet Rain Delay

If you're ready to start a healthy habit, juicing is a wonderful idea. The sweet potato in this drink will give it a new tasteful flavor you will enjoy.

Benefits:

Medical studies have shown that including beets in your diet help protect your body against heart disease. They also help regenerate red blood cells and supply fresh oxygen to the body.

Ingredients:

- Apple - 1 medium 180g
- Beet Root - 1 beet 170g
- Lemon - 1/2 fruit 42g
- Oranges (peeled) - 2 fruit 262g
- Sweet Potato - 1 130g

How to prepare:

- **Wash all the ingredients thoroughly.**
- **Juice them well and enjoy this fresh drink right away.**

Total calories: 245

Vitamins: Vitamin A 450ug, Vitamin C 87mg, Calcium 137mg

Minerals: Sodium 227mg, Potassium 1894mg

Sugars 34g

15. Rainbow Parade

The world of science is still discovering new things about how important vegetables and fruits are to our lives. Here is a great example of a juice recipe that will make you want to add them to your everyday meals.

Benefits:

A recent study has shown that foods rich in magnesium and fiber help the body drop blood pressure to healthier levels. Spinach is a great blood builder and regenerates red cells.

Ingredients:

- Celery - 4 stalk, medium 160g
- Cucumber - 1/2 cucumber 150g
- Grapes - 2 cup 180g
- Spinach - 4 cup 120g

How to prepare:

- **Wash all the ingredients thoroughly.**
- **Juice them well and enjoy this fresh drink right away.**

Total calories: 219

Vitamins: Vitamin A 322ug, Vitamin C 37mg, Calcium 179mg

Minerals: Sodium 144mg, Potassium 1671mg

Sugars 38g

16. Smiling Pineapple Mix

Here is another recipe that you should try. Share it with your family because it's really an amazing one if you like pineapple.

Benefits:

Drinking lemon juice is great for the heart and it also helps controls high blood pressure. A carrot a day reduces stroke risk by about 66 percent.

Ingredients:

- Carrots - 3 medium 180g
- Lemon - 1/2 fruit 40g
- Pineapple - 1/4 fruit 225g
- Spinach - 2 handful 50g

How to prepare:

- **Wash all the ingredients thoroughly.**
- **Juice them well and enjoy this fresh drink right away.**

Total calories: 202

Vitamins: Vitamin A 975ug, Vitamin C 150mg, Calcium 165mg

Minerals: Sodium 210mg, Potassium 1410mg

Sugars 37g

17. Cranberry Delight Juice

This juice recipe is unusual with a variety of ingredients you won't normally find anywhere so give it a try and notice the spectacular results you'll have.

Benefits:

Oranges being high in vitamin C can help stimulate white cells to fight different infections, and a recent study has linked them to lower blood pressure.

Ingredients:

- Cranberries - 3 cup, 300g
- Ginger Root - 2 thumb 45g
- Limes (with rind) - 2 fruit 134g
- Banana – 1 medium 90g

How to prepare:

- **Wash all the ingredients thoroughly.**
- **Juice them well and enjoy this fresh drink right away.**

Total calories: 285

Vitamins: Vitamin A 145ug, Vitamin C 219mg, Calcium 172mg

Minerals: Sodium 7mg, Potassium 1128mg

Sugars 48g

18. Kale Vow

Kale is full of necessary vitamins and minerals that will help your body reduce high blood pressure and make you feel much better during the day. Add some more leaves if you don't mind the added flavor as it will only make more nutritious.

Benefits:

Kale contains different compounds that lower high blood pressure and recent studies shown that lemons help in reducing cholesterol.

Ingredients:

- Apples - 2 medium 320g
- Kale - 2 leaf (8-12") 70g
- Lemon (peeled) - 1 fruit 58g
- Tomato - 1 medium whole 120g

How to prepare:

- **Wash all the ingredients thoroughly.**
- **Juice them well and enjoy this fresh drink right away.**

Total calories: 275

Vitamins: Vitamin A 434ug, Vitamin C 91mg, Calcium 201mg

Minerals: Sodium 190mg, Potassium 1448mg

Sugars 45g

19. Carroty Lime Max

This is a great juice to serve after or during a big meal. The combination of lime and pepper give it a kick in flavor but the banana makes it sweet tasting. If you feel it is still too strong in flavor simply add half a banana more.

Benefits:

Regular consumption of carrots reduces cholesterol levels and to prevent heart related problems. They also help cleanse the liver.

Ingredients:

- Carrots - 2 large 170g
- Celery - 2 stalk, large 128g
- Lime - 1/2 fruit 32g
- Pepper - 1 pepper 14g
- Spinach - 2 cup 60g
- Banana – 1 medium 90g

How to prepare:

- **Wash all the ingredients thoroughly.**
- **Juice them well and enjoy this fresh drink right away.**

Total calories: 110

Vitamins: Vitamin A 875ug, Vitamin C 32mg, Calcium 127mg

Minerals: Sodium 255mg, Potassium 1329mg

Sugars 15g

20. Cucumber High

If having a healthy body is your goal you have to try this juice recipe. You can lower the amount of onion if you don't like the flavor but it would be recommended you keep it in because of the health benefits.

Benefits:

Parsley has been shown to function as antioxidant and help maintain a healthy level of blood pressure. Tomato juice is an excellent source of vitamin C, calcium and phosphorous.

Ingredients:

- Cucumber - 1 cucumber 300g
- Lemon - 1 fruit 55g
- Onion - 15g
- Parsley - 1 handful 40g
- Tomatoes - 2 small whole 180g

How to prepare:

- **Wash all the ingredients thoroughly.**
- **Juice them well and enjoy this fresh drink right away.**

Total calories: 79

Vitamins: Vitamin A 255ug, Vitamin C 105mg, Calcium 98mg

Minerals: Sodium 30mg, Potassium 1077mg

Sugars 10g

21. Broc Mix

Let's see if this delicious juice recipe is what you are looking for. One of the great things about juice recipes is that they don't take much time to prepare and the results are outstanding.

Benefits:

Broccoli helps in proper functioning of insulin and regulates blood sugar, thereby regulating blood pressure also.

Ingredients:

- Apple - 1 medium 180g
- Broccoli - 1 stalk 150g
- Carrots - 2 large 110g
- Celery - 3 stalk, large 190g
- Olive Oil - 1 tablespoon 13.5g

How to prepare:

- **Wash all the ingredients thoroughly.**
- **Juice them well and enjoy this fresh drink right away.**

Total calories: 224

Vitamins: Vitamin A 1003ug, Vitamin C 110mg, Calcium 196mg

Minerals: Sodium 215mg, Potassium 1335mg

Sugars 19g

22. Blueberry Surprise Mix

Blueberries taste great and are wonderful anti-oxidants. Mixing these ingredients will give you a great juice to drink at any time of the day not just the morning.

Benefits:

Vitamins make our system function properly and are found in abundance in blueberries. Blueberries also help to maintain a strong immune system.

Ingredients:

- Apple - 1 medium 180g
- Blueberry - 1 cup 140g
- Broccoli - 1 stalk 151g
- Tomato - 1 medium whole 120g

How to prepare:

- **Wash all the ingredients thoroughly.**
- **Juice them well and enjoy this fresh drink right away.**

Total calories: 203

Vitamins: Vitamin A 784ug, Vitamin C 102mg, Calcium 115mg

Minerals: Sodium 188mg, Potassium 1431mg

Sugars 39g

23. Fit Ginger Juice

Here is another great juice recipe that you can enjoy at any moment of the day, just make sure you prepare it with 30 minutes before any big meal.

Benefits:

Pectin in carrots lowers the serum cholesterol levels and is also rich in vitamin A which is good for improving eyesight.

Ingredients:

- Carrots - 2 medium 120g
- Ginger Root - 1/2 12g
- Lemon - 1 fruit 50g
- Spinach - 2 handful 50g

How to prepare:

- **Wash all the ingredients thoroughly.**
- **Juice them well and enjoy this fresh drink right away.**

Total calories: 190

Vitamins: Vitamin A 1059ug, Vitamin C 71mg, Calcium 161mg

Minerals: Sodium 192mg, Potassium 1430mg

Sugars 31g

24. Orange Banana Mix

This is a wonderful juice for people who have serious problems with blood pressure and heart issues. The ingredients in this juice are packed with nutrients that will help strengthen your immune system as well.

Benefits:

Oranges, being high in flavonoids and vitamin C have been known to lower the risk of heart disease. A flavonoid called hesperidin found in oranges can lower high blood pressure.

Ingredients:

- Apples - 2 medium 360g
- Ginger Root - 1/2 thumb 12g
- Lime- ½ 30g
- Orange (peeled) - 1 fruit 130g
- Banana – 1 medium 90g

How to prepare:

- **Wash all the ingredients thoroughly.**
- **Juice them well and enjoy this fresh drink right away.**

Total calories: 166

Vitamins: Vitamin A 15ug, Vitamin C 71mg, Calcium 115mg

Minerals: Sodium 85mg, Potassium 982mg

Sugars 34g

25. Grapefruit Heart Disease Preventor

This is a great juice to help you prevent blood pressure and heart issues. Grapefruit is a powerful fruit with cholesterol lowering properties. You can add the entire fruit if you don't mind the flavor as it will make it even better for you and your heart.

Benefits:

Including celery in your diet helps protect the body against heart disease and also lowers blood pressure. Carrots have a cleansing effect on the liver and helps it to release more bile.

Ingredients:

- Apple - 1 large 200g
- Grapefruit - 1/2 large peeled 160g
- Beet Root - 1 beet 175g
- Carrots - 4 medium 244g
- Celery - 1 stalk, large 60g

How to prepare:

- **Wash all the ingredients thoroughly.**
- **Juice them well and enjoy this fresh drink right away.**

Total calories: 175

Vitamins: Vitamin A 1632ug, Vitamin C 38mg, Calcium 181mg

Minerals: Sodium 398mg, Potassium 1651mg

Sugars 33g

26. PomePower

Pomegranate is a delicious fruit that will add a distinctive flavor to this juice when added to the other ingredients. Try it morning or afternoon but not recommended for the evening.

Benefits:

Lemon juice helps control high blood pressure and prevents mental stress and depression.

Ingredients:

- Blueberry - 1 cup 145g
- Lemon – 1/2 fruit 30g
- Pomegranate - 1 pomegranate 280g
- Banana – 1 medium 100g

How to prepare:

- **Wash all the ingredients thoroughly.**
- **Juice them well and enjoy this fresh drink right away.**

Total calories: 176

Vitamins: Vitamin A 4ug, Vitamin C 42mg, Calcium 27mg

Minerals: Sodium 6mg, Potassium 580mg

Sugars 35g

27. A Plus Start

What a combination of vitamins and minerals in this juice! Kale and spinach together in one drink is spectacular. Make sure you drink this juice at least once per week.

Benefits:

People who eat two apples per day lower their cholesterol by as much as 15 percent. Apples might also lower blood pressure.

Ingredients:

- Apples - 2 medium 360g
- Kale - 2 leaf 70g
- Spinach - 2 cups 50g
- Lime – ½ fruit 30g

How to prepare:

- **Wash all the ingredients thoroughly.**
- **Juice them well and enjoy this fresh drink right away.**

Total calories: 132

Vitamins: Vitamin A 453ug, Vitamin C 87mg, Calcium 126mg

Minerals: Sodium 51mg, Potassium 815mg

Sugars 25g

28. Carrot Cut

Taste this juice recipe and you will be amazed of how delicious it is, and let's not forget all those vital nutrients that come together. It's a must for people with hypertension.

Benefits:

Pectin in carrots lowers the serum cholesterol levels and some studies show that they might play a role in lowering blood pressure.

Ingredients:

- Apples - 2 medium 360g
- Carrots - 2 medium 120g
- Ginger Root - 1/2 thumb 12g
- Cucumber -1 small 200g

How to prepare:

- **Wash all the ingredients thoroughly.**
- **Juice them well and enjoy this fresh drink right away.**

Total calories: 185

Vitamins: Vitamin A 750ug, Vitamin C 25mg, Calcium 54mg

Minerals: Sodium 48mg, Potassium 609mg

Sugars 27g

29. Peach Adore

It doesn't matter what time of the day it is, this juice recipe can be served at any hour. Check out all the ingredients and get ready for a delicious juice with a truly fantastic flavor.

Benefits:

Peaches might help in maintaining a balanced blood pressure level and also in being a blood purifier.

Ingredients:

- Carrots - 3 medium 130gg
- Lemon - 1/2 fruit 42g
- Peaches - 5 medium 750g
- Orange- 1 medium 120g

How to prepare:

- **Wash all the ingredients thoroughly.**
- **Juice them well and enjoy this fresh drink right away.**

Total calories: 362

Vitamins: Vitamin A 520ug, Vitamin C 71mg, Calcium 215mg

Minerals: Sodium 401mg, Potassium 3024mg

Sugars 7g

30. Sweet P

Here is another great tasting juice with sweet potato that is full of vitamins and minerals. It's very high on beta carotene which is fundamental in preventing hypertension and skin problems.

Benefits:

Sweet potatoes are a good source of nutrients and beets have been shown to help cleanse the blood.

Ingredients:

- Apples - 2 medium 364g
- Beet Root - 1 beet 82g
- Sweet Potato - 1 sweet potato, 130g
- Banana – 1 medium 100g

How to prepare:

- **Wash all the ingredients thoroughly.**
- **Juice them well and enjoy this fresh drink right away.**

Total calories: 201

Vitamins: Vitamin A 640ug, Vitamin C 16mg, Calcium 53mg

Minerals: Sodium 420mg, Potassium 3105mg

Sugars 30g

31. Pineapple Orange Mix

A healthy mind and a healthy body should be the motto of every individual. Add or reduce the amount of ginger root and kale depending on your preference.

Benefits:

Oranges have been shown to help lower blood pressure, and ginger lowers cholesterol.

Ingredients:

- Ginger Root - 1/2 thumb 12g
- Kale - 4 leaf 140g
- Orange - 1 small 96g
- Pineapple - 1 cup, chunks 165g
- Cucumber - 1 300g

How to prepare:

- **Wash all the ingredients thoroughly.**
- **Juice them well and enjoy this fresh drink right away.**

Total calories: 250

Vitamins: Vitamin A 594ug, Vitamin C 241mg, Calcium 203mg

Minerals: Sodium 39mg, Potassium 1160mg

Sugars 40g

32. Beet Peach Sabore

What's more important than your own health? Take the time to feed your body all the right vitamins and nutrients it needs with this great juice mix. Don't pay attention to the color of the drink as the flavor is what will make the difference.

Benefits:

The high content of iron in beets regenerates and reactivates the red blood cells. They also normalize blood pressure by lowering or elevating it.

Ingredients:

- Apple - 1 medium 180g
- Beet Root - 1 beet 82g
- Lemon - 1/2 fruit 29g
- Peach -1 medium 120g

How to prepare:

- **Wash all the ingredients thoroughly.**
- **Juice them well and enjoy this fresh drink right away.**

Total calories: 180

Vitamins: Vitamin A 10ug, Vitamin C 101mg, Calcium 45mg

Minerals: Sodium 44mg, Potassium 760mg

Sugars 39g

33. Spinach Punch

Juicing has become a very popular way of getting healthy, but is not as popular as it will be in the future. Be a step ahead of everyone by juicing your way to a more controlled blood pressure level with this spinach mix.

Benefits:

Ginger Root is great for lowering blood pressure and reducing the risk of cancer.

Ingredients:

- Apples - 1 medium 180g
- Carrots - 2 medium 120g
- Ginger Root - 1/2 thumb 12g
- Lime - 1 fruit 55g
- Spinach – 2 handful 50g

How to prepare:

- **Wash all the ingredients thoroughly.**
- **Juice them well and enjoy this fresh drink right away.**

Total calories: 193

Vitamins: Vitamin A 1785ug, Vitamin C 98 mg, Calcium 94mg

Minerals: Sodium 156mg, Potassium 1459mg

Sugars 33g

34. FB Health Mix

Your own health should be treated seriously. Having high blood pressure is serious and should be watched carefully. This juice is a great start towards maintaining your blood pressure stabilized.

Benefits:

Drinking Fennel Bulb juice is helpful for people suffering with heart problems as it contains potassium. Ginger can increase blood circulation and combat fever.

Ingredients:

- Apples - 2 medium 360g
- Fennel Bulb (with fronds) - 1 bulb 230g
- Ginger Root - 1/2 thumb 12g
- Orange (peeled) - 1 fruit 130g

How to prepare:

- **Wash all the ingredients thoroughly.**
- **Juice them well and enjoy this fresh drink right away.**

Total calories: 153

Vitamins: Vitamin A 15ug, Vitamin C 70mg, Calcium 118mg

Minerals: Sodium 79mg, Potassium 1144mg

Sugars 31g

35. Beet Fast

A good solution for any type of health problem is adding fruits and vegetables to your juice recipes. Check out the benefits and all the ingredients you will get from this juice and the different flavor from the parsley.

Benefits:

Parsley has been used in animal studies to help increase the antioxidant capacity of the blood. Beets are useful in helping cleanse the liver, and the liver helps metabolize fat.

Ingredients:

- Apple - 1 medium 180g
- Beet Root - 1/2 beet 40g
- Carrots - 3 medium 180g
- Parsley - 1 handful 40g
- Lime – ½ 30g

How to prepare:

- **Wash all the ingredients thoroughly.**
- **Juice them well and enjoy this fresh drink right away.**

Total calories: 119

Vitamins: Vitamin A 1174ug, Vitamin C 45mg, Calcium 121mg

Minerals: Sodium 190mg, Potassium 1005mg

Sugars 22g

36. Pine A Plus Juice

The combination of pineapple and apple make this juice taste delicious and the other ingredients bring added vitamins that it a great choice to start the day or any time of the day.

Benefits:

Pineapple juice is rich in vitamins and it might help lower blood pressure and even reduce cholesterol levels.

Ingredients:

- Apple - 1 medium 180g
- Lemon - 1/2 fruit 25g
- Orange (peeled) - 1 large 180g
- Pineapple - 1/4 fruit 225g
- Cucumber – 1 300g

How to prepare:

- **Wash all the ingredients thoroughly.**
- **Juice them well and enjoy this fresh drink right away.**

Total calories: 215

Vitamins: Vitamin A 41ug, Vitamin C 140mg, Calcium 90mg

Minerals: Sodium 5mg, Potassium 837mg

Sugars 49g

37. Double Mango Orange

As your body grows older if you don't take care of it, you might encounter different problems. One of them being high blood pressure. This juice recipe will help you to control your hypertension and prevent other future health problems.

Benefits:

Oranges, being high in vitamin C can help stimulate white cells to fight infection, naturally building a good immune system. Mango can help reduce cholesterol.

Ingredients:

- Apple - 1 large 223g
- Lemon (peeled) - 1/2 fruit 29g
- Mango (peeled) - 1 fruit 336g
- Orange - 1 large 184g
- Spinach – 50g

How to prepare:

- **Wash all the ingredients thoroughly.**
- **Juice them well and enjoy this fresh drink right away.**

Total calories: 245

Vitamins: Vitamin A 146ug, Vitamin C 147mg, Calcium 91mg

Minerals: Sodium 4mg, Potassium 860mg

Sugars 50g

38. Orangy Delight

Try this juice recipe and see how the benefits will change the way you feel and perform during the day. You will see after the first day you won't want to miss it another day.

Benefits:

Carrots do wonders for boosting the immune system by increasing the production and performance of white blood cells. Oranges can lower high blood pressure.

Ingredients:

- Apples - 2 large 400g
- Carrots - 5 medium 200g
- Orange - 1 large 184g
- Peaches - 2 large 350g
- Banana – 1 medium 100g

How to prepare:

- **Wash all the ingredients thoroughly.**
- **Juice them well and enjoy this fresh drink right away.**

Total calories: 379

Vitamins: Vitamin A 3376ug, Vitamin C 116mg, Calcium 220mg

Minerals: Sodium 291mg, Potassium 2521mg

Sugars 80g

39. Cranberry Light

This juice recipe is great to server at the end of the day, because it will make your body relax faster before going to bed. It will also supply you with a lot of the vitamins and minerals you will need to start the next day.

Benefits:

Cranberries are a great source of vitamins and minerals. They lower blood pressure and improve blood circulation.

Ingredients:

- Apples - 3 medium 546g
- Cranberries - 1/2 cup, whole 50g
- Ginger Root - 1/4 thumb 6g
- Orange - 1 large (184g
- Lime – ½ fruit 25 g
- Spinach – 50g

How to prepare:

- **Wash all the ingredients thoroughly.**
- **Juice them well and enjoy this fresh drink right away.**

Total calories: 220

Vitamins: Vitamin A 23ug, Vitamin C 87mg, Calcium 80mg

Minerals: Sodium 5mg, Potassium 725mg

Sugars 41g

40. Reduce Stress Mix

If stress is your problem, then you should see what effects this juice recipe will have on you. It's really great and you won't stress about your health as much now that you're getting an overload of nutrients.

Benefits:

Celery calms the nerves because of the high calcium content & helps in controlling high blood pressure. Raw celery should be eaten to reduce high blood pressure.

Ingredients:

- Apple - 1 medium 180g
- Celery - 2 stalk, large 120gg
- Lemon (with peel) - 1/2 fruit 42g
- Banana – 1 medium 100g

How to prepare:

- **Wash all the ingredients thoroughly.**
- **Juice them well and enjoy this fresh drink right away.**

Total calories: 128

Vitamins: Vitamin A 101ug, Vitamin C 87mg, Calcium 140mg

Minerals: Sodium 124mg, Potassium 1027mg

Sugars 19g

41. B Victory

This juice recipe should be on the top of your list. It has a great content of vitamins and minerals. The best time of the day to serve it would be in the morning because it will give you a big energy boost.

Benefits:

Beets are high in carbohydrates, meaning they are a great instant energy source. They are a good blood purifier.

Ingredients:

- Apple - 1 large 200g
- Beet Root - 1 beet 170g
- Carrots - 4 medium 241g
- Celery - 1 stalk, large 60g

How to prepare:

- **Wash all the ingredients thoroughly.**
- **Juice them well and enjoy this fresh drink right away.**

Total calories: 155

Vitamins: Vitamin A 1292ug, Vitamin C 34mg, Calcium 175mg

Minerals: Sodium 300mg, Potassium 1750mg

Sugars 30g

42. Double AA Gulp

After you serve a meal you should wait 30-60 minutes before you can drink this juice recipe. Check the ingredients and how to prepare it before starting. Get ready for a delicious and very healthy source of vitamins and minerals.

Benefits:

Avocados reduce risk of heart disease and help the immune system get stronger.

Ingredients:

- Apples – 1 medium 150g
- Avocado - 1 avocado 188g
- Lime - 1 fruit 60g
- Spinach - 2 cup 60g

How to prepare:

- **Wash all the ingredients thoroughly.**
- **Juice them well and enjoy this fresh drink right away.**

Total calories: 353

Vitamins: Vitamin A 243ug, Vitamin C 47mg, Calcium 164mg

Minerals: Sodium 152mg, Potassium 1788mg

Sugars 20g

43. BALK Juice

If you want to start controlling your hypertension in a fast and effective way, then you should begin with this juice. It's easy to prepare and has a high source of antioxidants necessary to prevent all kinds of diseases.

Benefits:

Several nutrients contained in kiwifruit, including iron, copper and vitamins. Studies indicate that it might help reduce heart disease.

Ingredients:

- Blackberry - 1 cup 120g
- Kiwifruit - 1 fruit 69g
- Apple -2 large 360 g
- Lime – ½ 30 g

How to prepare:

- **Wash all the ingredients thoroughly.**
- **Juice them well and enjoy this fresh drink right away.**

Total calories: 183

Vitamins: Vitamin A 80ug, Vitamin C 110mg, Calcium 75mg

Minerals: Sodium 7mg, Potassium 560mg

Sugars 30g

44. Daily Double Mix

Indeed a healthy lifestyle should consist of doing daily exercises and taking care of your diet. That's why juice recipe should be taken often and in the morning to help you start off your day with a strong dose of beta-carotene.

Benefits:

Celery and apples help lowering high blood pressure, and they are an excellent source of nutrients.

Ingredients:

- 2 large Carrots, 200g
- Tomatoes -1 medium 110g
- Apple – 1 medium 100g
- Celery -1 stalk 50g

How to prepare:

- **Wash all the ingredients thoroughly.**
- **Juice them together and enjoy this fresh drink right away.**

Total calories: 163

Vitamins: Vitamin A 400μg, Vitamin C 15mg, Calcium 20mg

Minerals: Sodium 13mg, Potassium 223 mg

Sugars 15g

45. Tangy Potato

If you were looking for something that can help blood pressure health problems you should see how this juice recipe is prepared and give it a try. You might want to take it in the morning but can also drink it during the day. It looks great and tastes even better because of all the sweet ingredients it has.

Benefits:

Oranges are a great source of vitamins and may also help in reducing high blood pressure.

Ingredients:

- Apples – 2, 360g
- Celery - 1 stalk, 65g
- Orange (peeled) - 125g
- Sweet Potato - 120g
- Banana – 1 medium 100g

How to prepare:

- **Wash all the ingredients thoroughly.**
- **Juice them together and enjoy this fresh drink right away.**

Total calories: 330

Vitamins: Vitamin A 690μg, Vitamin C 75mg, Calcium 150mg

Minerals: Sodium 76mg, Potassium 349mg

Sugars 55g

46. Power Kick

There are plenty of juice recipes that will bring positive results to your health but this one will is specific for hypertension. You can eliminate the lime if you feel it give it a flavor too strong for your palate.

Benefits:

Carrots increase performance of white blood cells and help eliminate excess fluids from the body. Blood pressure is reduced also by them.

Ingredients:

- Carrots - 2 medium 120g
- Celery - 1 stalk, 50g
- Tomatoes - 2 medium whole 220g
- Banana – 1 medium 100g
- Lime – ½ 25g

How to prepare:

- **Wash all the ingredients thoroughly.**
- **Juice them together and enjoy this fresh drink right away.**

Total calories: 85

Vitamins: Vitamin A 900µg, Vitamin C 140mg, Calcium 197mg

Minerals: Sodium 24mg, Potassium 268mg

Sugars 14g

47. Maximum Strength Mix

This juice recipe is great to serve in the morning because of the strong taste it has and the wonderful effects it will have over your body throughout the day. You can add or reduce the portions to satisfy your needs and to make it to your liking.

Benefits:

Apples are a great source of vitamins and they are also known for lowering high blood pressure and a high content of nutrients.

Ingredients:

- Apples -1 large – 120g
- Ginger Root - 45g
- Grapefruit (peeled)- 300g

How to prepare:

- **Wash all the ingredients thoroughly.**
- **Juice them together and enjoy this fresh drink right away.**

Total calories: 220

Vitamins: Vitamin A 123μg, Vitamin C 200mg, Calcium 139mg

Minerals: Sodium 9mg, Potassium 220mg

Sugars 42g

48. Strawberry Punch Mix

This juice is very high in vitamin C because of all the strawberries that are in it as well as the lemon. The carrots add beta-carotene to the added benefits which makes this an awesome drink.

Benefits:

Strawberries help lower cancer death rates, and are known for lowering the risk of heart disease.

Ingredients:

- Apples – 1 large 120g
- Lemon - 1/2 fruit 32g
- Strawberries - 2 cup, 230g
- Carrot - 1 small, 50g

How to prepare:

- **Wash all the ingredients thoroughly.**
- **Juice them together and enjoy this fresh drink right away.**

Total calories: 190

Vitamins: Vitamin A 11μg, Vitamin C 185mg, Calcium 68mg

Minerals: Sodium 4mg, Potassium 850mg

Sugars 40g

49. Extra Energy Juice

We all know how vegetables and fruits are very healthy for our body that is why you should start drinking juice recipes that contain a large variety of them but with great flavor. This is an unusual drink and can be adapted if you don't like any of the ingredients as it does have a strong flavor.

Benefits:

Studies have shown that Cranberries might lower blood pressure and they are good to boost the immune system.

Ingredients:

- Brussel Sprout – 1 sprout 17g
- Cucumber -1, 300g
- Pineapple – ¼ 220g
- Spinach – 2 handful 50g
- Cranberries – 2 cup 190g

How to prepare:

- **Wash all the ingredients thoroughly.**
- **Juice them together and enjoy this fresh drink right away.**

Total calories: 150

Vitamins: Vitamin A 410μg, Vitamin C 204mg, Calcium 209mg

Minerals: Sodium 79mg, Potassium 470mg

Sugars 34g

50. BOAP Juice

Having time restricted lifestyles and busy days is no excuse for not focusing on controlling your high blood pressure so make sure you do what's necessary to drink your way top better health on a consistent basis.

Benefits:

Oranges being high in vitamin C reduce the risk of heart diseases, and also might lower blood pressure levels.

Ingredients:

- Applet - 1 medium 180g
- Oranges - 2 large 365g
- Peaches - 2 medium 300g
- Banana – 1 medium 120g

How to prepare:

- **Wash all the ingredients thoroughly.**
- **Juice them together and enjoy this fresh drink right away.**

Total of calories: 940

Vitamins: Vitamin A 50µg, Vitamin C 110mg, Calcium 100mg

Minerals: Sodium 30mg, Potassium 120mg

Sugars 40g

OTHER GREAT TITLES BY THIS AUTHOR

Advanced Mental Toughness Training for Bodybuilders

Using Visualization to Push Yourself to the Limit

By

Joseph Correa

Certified Sports Nutritionist

Becoming Mentally Tougher in Bodybuilding by Using Meditation

Reach Your Potential by Controlling Your Inner Thoughts

By

Joseph Correa

Certified Sports Nutritionist

www.ingramcontent.com/pod-product-compliance
Lightning Source LLC
Chambersburg PA
CBHW070139080526
44586CB00015B/1755